Solids, Liquids, and Gases

by **Daniel Shepard**

With the Editors of TIME FOR KIDS

Macmillan
McGraw-Hill

These blocks are **solid**.

A solid keeps its shape
until something changes it.

Water is a **liquid**.
Milk is a liquid, too.

A liquid takes the shape
of what you pour it into.

Air is a **gas**.
Gas spreads out to fill space.

The world is filled with solids, liquids, and gases.

Glossary

 gas (GAS) matter that spreads out to fill space *(page 6)*

 liquid (LIK-wid) matter that takes the shape of what you pour it into *(page 4)*

 solid (SOL-id) matter that has its own shape *(page 2)*

Index